PRAISE

"[These pointers] are powerfully pithy and practically profound. Sims is a master at giving the best presentation advice in very digestible chunks."   —Patricia Fripp, former president, National Speakers Association

"The talented Sims Wyeth is a breath of fresh air in a world of ponderous teachers and all-knowing lecturers. Long may he assist clients!"   —Charles Reilly, chairman, In-Person Communications

"Sims Wyeth is a master of effective and persuasive presentations. It's no surprise then, that his book is an object example: clear, insightful, wise—and a delight to read."
    —Charles Green, president, Trusted Advisor

"One of the best presentation coaches I know . . . Wyeth comes up with dozens of *koan*-like tips on how to be a more persuasive public speaker and effective presenter."   —*Inc. Magazine*

"This book is the next best thing to having Sims on your left shoulder as you go into a meeting or presentation."
    —Charles van Horne, managing director, Abbott Capital

"Whether you are a seasoned veteran or a neophyte public speaker; whether you are creating a presentation or giving one; whether you are full of courage or tim

Garfield County Libraries
Carbondale Branch Library
320 Sopris Avenue
Carbondale, CO 81623
(970) 963-2889 • Fax (970) 963-8573
www.GCPLD.org

Persuasive Public Speaking is a must-read. Sims Wyeth takes his over-twenty years of experience in the art of skillful speaking and synthesizes everything you need to know into an easy-to-read and inspirational set of dos and don'ts. If you like getting your point across; if you like winning the attention and admiration of a crowd; and if you like the thrill of making things happen when you stand up to speak, get this book, and cease your sweating evermore."
—Mike Blechar,
former vice president, Gartner

"What a wonderful collection of insights, hints, and tips! In a more formal age we would only receive this wisdom after swearing loyalty to a secret society, a guild. But here now for anyone who wishes to become a better speaker, Wyeth shares his distillation of decades of work, thousands of conversations, years of teaching and learning the practice of speech."
—William Malik, founder of Malik Consulting

"I am delighted that Sims Wyeth has compiled his pithy advice on successful public speaking. For years I have been printing out each oratorical *bon mot*, and now I will have a single source to refer to when contemplating my next appearance on a dais."
—John Bliss, founder, Bliss PR

Garfield County Libraries

The

ESSENTIALS
of PERSUASIVE
PUBLIC
SPEAKING

SIMS WYETH

W. W. NORTON & COMPANY

NEW YORK / LONDON

The
ESSENTIALS
of PERSUASIVE
PUBLIC
SPEAKING

Copyright © 2014, 2011 by Sims Wyeth

Previous edition published under the title *A Zen Monk Had Sweaty Palms: Pointers on the Path to Better Public Speaking*

All rights reserved
Printed in the United States of America

For information about permission to reproduce selections from this book, write to Permissions, W. W. Norton & Company, Inc., 500 Fifth Avenue, New York, NY 10110

For information about special discounts for bulk purchases, please contact W. W. Norton Special Sales at specialsales@wwnorton.com or 800-233-4830

Manufacturing by Courier Westford
Book design by Ellen Cipriano
Production manager: Louise Mattarelliano

Library of Congress Cataloging-in-Publication Data

Wyeth, Sims.
[Zen Monk Had Sweaty Palms]
The essentials of persuasive public speaking / Sims Wyeth.
pages cm
Previous edition published under the title "A Zen Monk Had Sweaty Palms: Pointers on the Path to Better Public Speaking."
ISBN 978-0-393-34604-6 (pbk.)
1. Public speaking. 2. Oral communication. I. Title.
PN4129.15.W94 2014
808.5'1—dc23

                    2013034799

W. W. Norton & Company, Inc.
500 Fifth Avenue, New York, N.Y. 10110
www.wwnorton.com

W. W. Norton & Company Ltd.
Castle House, 75/76 Wells Street, London W1T 3QT

1 2 3 4 5 6 7 8 9 0

To my wife, Sharon,

my daughter, Georgie,

and in memory of my parents, Nancy and Buz Wyeth

CONTENTS

■   ■   ■

ACKNOWLEDGMENTS

■   ■   ■

The following people have contributed to this book directly or indirectly:

Marian Rich

Graham Bernard

Blair Cutting

Beatrice Straight

Deirdre Hurst DuPrey

Robert Lloyd

Peter Giuliano

Frank Carillo

Charles Reilly

Beth Smith

Andrea Knapp Peiser

Diane Klein

Francis Klein

Sharon Dennis Wyeth

Georgie Wyeth

Buz Wyeth

Starling Lawrence

Jeff Shreve

PRAISE NO MAN BEFORE HE SPEAKS,
FOR IT IS THEN THAT MEN ARE TESTED.

—The Book of Sirach,
Chapter 27, verses 6–7

INTRODUCTION

■　　■　　■

ON THE DAY you ascend into heaven, take a few minutes to sit on a cloud and add up the hours you spent giving presentations or speaking publicly. The total will be a small fraction of your time on earth.

However, those few occasions may well have had a disproportionate impact on your professional success, and quite possibly on the fullness of your life. Why?

Because, unless you're a famous artist, you give more to others through your speech than through any other form of communication, because you know more than you can say, but you can say more than you can write.

And, if you are a knowledge worker, someone who makes a living with words and numbers, your career depends on how you speak, write, and think—in that order—because nobody knows what you think until you speak or write, and, these days, few of us read. We skim, we scan, we surf, but mostly we wait for the meeting. We wait for the presentation, when a speaker turns information into meaning, and imprints that meaning on our minds through the power of story.

This book contains short pointers on presenting and public speaking. You can consume them randomly, serially, or topically. They come out of my fascination with speech, my respect for those who can do it well, and my own ambition to be confident, persuasive, and engaging.

I've tried to make all the pointers substantive and fun, like organic jalapeño potato chips, so you'll consume them one after the other. Most of them tell you what to do or not to do when preparing and delivering speeches or presentations.

Occasionally a pointer escapes from the realm of the practical and lights out for the territory of the general and the abstract, but I've tried to keep the number of runaways to a minimum.

Public speaking is a centripetal social force: it pulls people into the same place at the same time to think about the same thing. It is an ancient technology designed to help tribes, communities, companies, and nations make wise decisions.

Good leaders generally speak well, but not all good speakers are good leaders. Demagogues, despots, and egotists abound.

The world needs you to be a good leader who speaks well, and a good adviser to leaders.

I hope my pointers are helpful.

Sims Wyeth
Montclair, New Jersey

The
POWER *of*
SPEECH

SUSPEND THEIR DISBELIEF

■   ■   ■

WHEN I WAS A CHILD in Katonah, New York, I had a recurring dream that I stood atop the Cross River Dam and said powerful and eloquent things to people off in the distance.

The dream foretold my future. I became an actor and spoke the poetry of Shakespeare before becoming a professor of theater and then a consultant to business leaders.

Theater and business have something in common. In both, you get paid for your performance. And those who get paid the most are endowed, or acquire through study and experience, the ability to create in others the willing suspension of disbelief.

That, in a nutshell, is the job of the actor and of the business speaker.

MAKE IT PERSONAL

■ ■ ■

LIKE MANY YOUNG PEOPLE who value authenticity and watch their pennies, my twenty-eight-year-old daughter does not buy greeting cards. She makes her own.

I have quite a collection of them, including this from a recent Christmas:

> *Your spirit outweighs*
> > *Your burden:*
> > *One hundred calls*
> > *Each old day. Fresh hands.*

I have it taped to the wall in my office, for inspiration when I'm cold-calling.

Hallmark makes good cards, but I've never put one on my wall. Speech that authentically reveals the personality of the speaker, and is addressed to and about an individual or defined group, is far more memorable than a message from a corporation meant for a demographic.

Make all your presentations personal.

LET THERE BE DRAMA

■   ■   ■

MARCUS TULLIUS CICERO, the great Roman orator, said, "Tickling and soothing anxieties is the test of a speaker's impact and technique." He could have said the same about dramatists and storytellers.

We humans come together over drama. In the past, we gathered to hear stories around the fire, sagas of gods sung on a lyre, and the tragedies of great men with fatal flaws.

We're still doing it. We gather to watch plays, movies, and TV shows. We gather by the millions to watch sporting events, because the outcome is uncertain, and we stay up late to see what happens next.

A speaker should be a dramatist capable of capturing and holding attention by tickling, then soothing audience anxiety.

Let there be drama in your presentations.

FAKE IT 'TIL YOU MAKE IT

■　　■　　■

WHEN I ASK people to try a more expressive style—to be louder, or to get their hands above their waist, I often hear them say, "That's not my style," or, "That's just not me."

Limiting your definition of *self* must be comforting, but sometimes as a speaker you need to act not as you would habitually, but as you must to achieve your goals.

In other words, you need to fake it 'til you make it. Actors rehearse until they discover and become the character. You can practice new behaviors until they become more natural.

You may have fixed traits, but to grow as a speaker, sign a free-trait agreement with yourself.

HOW ABOUT SOME WISDOM?

■　　■　　■

I AM TIRED of expert speakers with expert opinions.
Everyone is an expert in something. I want a *wise* speaker.

I liked it when Peter Gomes, the minister at Harvard, said at a
graduation ceremony, "There is less going on here than meets
the eye."

And I was lit up for days after I read this Einstein quote
inscribed over a bar: "There are two ways to live. You can live
as if there is no such thing as a miracle, or you can live as if
everything is a miracle."

We put our trust in experts and they're often proved wrong.
Enough already with the experts. How about some wisdom?

SPOKEN BEATS WRITTEN

. . .

WRITTEN WORDS ARE the children of absent fathers: their dads aren't around to help them explain themselves.

Socrates complained about this problem: "If you question [written words], wanting to know about their sayings, they always say only one and the same thing."

Consider what questioning could have done for these headlines:

RED TAPE HOLDS UP NEW BRIDGE
Milford [CT] Citizen, July 12, 1982

DEFENDANT'S SPEECH ENDS IN LONG SENTENCE
Minneapolis Tribune, February 25, 1987

PANDA LECTURES THIS WEEK AT NATIONAL ZOO
The Washington Post, January 13, 2001

Spoken language is less ambiguous and more persuasive than written language because it is amplified and clarified by gesture, voice, character, and dialogue.

A ZEN MONK HAD
SWEATY PALMS

■   ■   ■

A ZEN MONK, always calm among commoners, noticed he had sweaty palms while officiating at a nobleman's wedding.

He returned to his monastery, told his disciples he was not fit to be their teacher, and left in search of enlightenment. Eight years later, he returned to resume his duties, serving with equanimity commoners and noblemen alike.

Your sameness of bearing in front of chairmen and workmen demonstrates your ability to speak to the sameness of being in all your listeners.

TONE IT DOWN

■ ■ ■

IN THE TWENTY-THREE YEARS I've been working with business speakers, I've had only one client to whom I had to say, "You've got to tone it down."

Passion is great, but not when it lacks decorum, not when it offends the tone of the occasion and distracts the audience from the message.

It was relatively easy for him to tone it down. Cutting back is easier than taking it up a notch.

PUBLIC SPEAKING
IS THE GLUE

■　　■　　■

PUBLIC SPEAKING IS the number one tool of leadership because when you get people in a room to hear the same message at the same time you have the greatest chance of moving them to action.

Don't waste your opportunities. The glue that holds people together is a magical mystery sauce of trust, emotion, and shared purpose. In business, meetings and presentations are key opportunities for creating and sustaining that magic.

WHY DO WE PRESENT?

■   ■   ■

WHY DON'T WE just hand in our report and call it a day?

Because we humans have been around in our present form for 200,000 years. If we envision those years along a yardstick, written language appears on the last two-thirds of the final inch of that stick, and widespread literacy on the last sixteenth of the final inch.

For 200,000 years, human groups have made important decisions based on the spoken word, testing not only the ideas under discussion but the character of those who propose them.

If you can move the minds of others, they see in you the ability to get things done, and they see that in your language and expression.

BE LOGICAL AND STYLISH

■　　■　　■

THE BEST BOOK I know about business presenting is *Moving Mountains* by Henry M. Boettinger, published by Macmillan in 1969.

Here are some quotes from the book:

> Cool clinical men may analyze an idea until it lies dead in their hands like a dissected frog. But even Hegel, that most academic of philosophers, acknowledged: "Nothing great has been accomplished without passion."

> Logic may be the language of reason, but style adds to it life, sentiment, shading, and judgment. Training teaches the rules, experience teaches the exceptions.

If you're a serious student of the art, find this book.

ASPIRE TO WEAR
THE CROWN

■   ■   ■

AS AN AUDIENCE grows in size, both the inhibition of the intellect and the intensification of emotions grow roughly in proportion. But in smaller groups, dialogue and detail become more important.

Most of us in business are better at talking about facts and figures than we are at evoking emotions, values, and beliefs. But the ability to unite both types of speaking—the intellectual and the emotional—is the jewel in the crown of public speech.

Aspire to wear the crown.

MAKE IT NEW AND FAMILIAR

■   ■   ■

GREAT IDEAS, presented well, can make the new familiar and the familiar new.

After centuries lit by candlelight, Thomas Edison gained acceptance for the electric bulb by shaping it like a flame.

With his wizardly product launches, Steve Jobs turned the clunky personal computer into a new kind of appliance—an object of utility, beauty, and status.

And then there's President Kennedy. The moon is new every month, but he made a man on the moon familiar.

Language lies close to the heart of invention.

THE ABCs OF PRESENTING

■   ■   ■

Thou shalt not be Arrogant.
Thou shalt not be Boring.
Thou shalt not be Confusing.

Let those of us who seek to sell ourselves, our ideas, and our products or services contemplate these ABCs, lest we be turned away . . .

by the prospect who decides to buy from our competitor,
by the client who rejects our advice,
or by our own bosses and colleagues, who would banish
   us from lofty executive perches,

because we violated one of the ABCs of highly effective speech.

STICK TO BEING YOU

■   ■   ■

WHAT WE EXPERIENCE in many situations depends to a great extent on what we have encountered immediately prior to that situation.

For instance, heat feels warmer when we come in from the cold. Light seems brighter when we emerge from the dark; silence, more silent when the noise suddenly stops.

When you are waiting your turn to speak, remember this: You are unique. You are different from the person who spoke before you and anyone who comes after you. You are a contrast, and as such you will be welcomed.

Stick to being you. Everyone else is taken.

FAIL YOUR WAY TO SUCCESS

■   ■   ■

SOME PEOPLE THINK that the ability to present effectively is innate—you either have it or you don't. Wrong! It is an art that can be learned by everyone, including the shy, the dull, and the inarticulate.

The stories are innumerable. Churchill fainted at his first speech in Parliament. As secretary of the navy, FDR bored people to tears. Bill Clinton was booed at the 1988 Democratic Convention for his long-windedness.

Yet all three are now known as brilliant communicators. They persisted and excelled. So can you.

BE THE SPEAKER YOUR DOG THINKS YOU ARE

■   ■   ■

AT THE RETIREMENT community where my parents lived, I saw a sign on an apartment door that read, "My ambition is to be the person my dog thinks I am."

That makes sense to me. As far as I can tell, my dog thinks I am authoritative, fun, and kind, and that's pretty much my ambition as a person—and as a speaker too.

When presenting, be the person your dog thinks you are.

BE A BEE

■　　■　　■

MY FATHER KEPT BEES. They lived in a little sub-development of hives out in the field behind the barn, pollinating my mother's flower gardens and yielding up their extra honey to many Mason jars.

Bees play a win-win game: they get pollen from flowers, which is the raw material for making honey, and the flowers get their seed spread. Bee business is sustainable.

Speakers can be honey bee–like. When they connect with their listeners, intellectually and emotionally, they gather attention, which is like nectar of the gods for a speaker.

And when listeners really listen, the seeds of knowledge carried by the speaker are more likely to take root and spread.

Sweet outcomes all around!

TO JUMP OR NOT TO JUMP

■   ■   ■

SUPPOSE I'M BEING CHASED by a psychotic killer, and I stand on a rock on the side of a raging stream and think about leaping across to the next rock. I calculate my chances of reaching that rock, and then I calculate the consequences of falling short and drowning in the torrent, or not leaping and getting axed by the psycho behind me.

This is real life. I can't do a statistical analysis. I have to make a decision now. And it's all done by some primordial gyroscopic mechanism that has something to do with thinking, but more to do with intuition.

Presentations help people to make decisions or predictions. Should we promote this guy or that gal? Buy this company, or buy another? Jump in the water, or turn and face the fight?

And when all the calculations are made, and the results are in, there's still a gap in our knowledge—a gap made of doubt. Decisions come down to a leap of faith, and high-stakes presentations are meant to convince an audience to jump or not to jump.

BE A TRIPLE THREAT

■ ■ ■

WHEN I WAS YOUNGER, and just starting out as a speaker and consultant, I needed a surface—a look—a suit and a haircut.

Once I had that, I needed the content and the context. I wanted to know everything about spoken communication, and I wanted to know about my clients' businesses.

Now I want to experience my own authenticity and my own truth. I want to speak more from my heart and less from my brain. I am less interested in *seeming* and more interested in *being*.

I suspect these phases are all necessary. You need a good first impression, knowledge born from experience, and finally, a sense of perspective about the limits of knowledge.

On Broadway, you're a triple threat if you can sing, dance, and act. In business, you're a triple threat if you look the part, know the part, and see your role in the larger drama.

QUALITY COMES FROM QUANTITY

■   ■   ■

THE PRESIDENT OF AVON told me one of her VPs boasted that he was very selective when admitting new Avon ladies to his division. She said she disagreed with him.

"Quality comes from quantity," she told me. "No one can predict who will be the next big winner. We should admit them all, see how they do, and in a while, we'll find the gems."

Accept every invitation to present. Seek out opportunities to speak. The more you speak to groups, the stronger you become.

Speak 10,000 times. Quality comes from quantity.

KEEP IT SIMPLE, SMARTY!

■ ■ ■

A SALES GUY, a marketer, and an analyst take a train from New York to Montreal. Crossing into Canada, they see a purple cow standing in a field.

"Look," says the sales guy, "Canadian cows are purple."

"No," says the marketer, "Probably *some* cows in Canada are purple."

The analyst looks pained. "No: In Canada, there is at least one field, containing at least one cow, at least one side of which is purple."

In this scenario, the analyst is thorough, precise, and accurate. The sales guy is drawing conclusions without adequate proof, but the marketing guy is stating a simple truth, a probability.

Most presentations get less effective when loaded with too many fine distinctions. As a speaker, you don't have to be mathematically exact. You have to deal only in probabilities.

GIVE RHETORIC ITS DUE

■ ■ ■

IN *Lectures on Rhetoric and Belles Lettres*, Hugh Blair (1718–1800), a Scottish teacher and minister, defended the dignity of rhetoric.

"Speech," he wrote, "is the great instrument by which man becomes beneficial to man; and it is to the intercourse and transmission of thought, by means of speech, that we are chiefly indebted for the improvement of thought itself."

Do you think of speeches as "hot air"? Are presentations "dog-and-pony shows?" Recall how you've won your clients, landed a job by acing an interview, or talked your way out of a traffic ticket.

You used rhetoric. You displayed through your speech trust-worthiness, expertise, and knowledge of your listener's needs.

Give rhetoric its due.

ALL VALUE IS
PERCEIVED VALUE

■   ■   ■

ADVERTISING ADDS TO the intrinsic value of products by enhancing our perception of them.

Your ability to present well adds perceived value to the intrinsic value of your content and character. People who look good, sound good, and make compelling sense in high-stakes moments have an unfair advantage over those who don't.

Do not dismiss the power of perception. All value is perceived value.

CUT A FIGURE

■   ■   ■

"IF YOU CAN give a decent speech in public or cut any kind of figure on the podium, then you never need to dine or sleep alone," said the late Christopher Hitchens, who was in the room at Oxford in the late 1960s when Bill Clinton didn't inhale.

Good speakers project confidence, a quality attractive in men and women. You probably have no need for random dinner partners or overnight guests, but I'm sure you'd like to make more money, get promoted, have more influence, feel more confident, and bask in the adoration of the crowd.

So go ahead, cut a figure on the podium.

GET OUT OF YOUR HEAD
AND INTO THEIRS

■   ■   ■

OUR MODELS OF the world are made of words, pictures, numbers, and beliefs. Yet the world often refuses to conform to our models. The map is not the terrain.

For instance, there was once a statistician who drowned while trying to wade across a river with an average depth of three feet.

The world we live in is created in our heads. The world our listeners live in is created in *their* heads, and that's the world we need to connect with.

BE HUMBLE, HUMOROUS,
AND BRIEF

■　　■　　■

I PULLED INTO a gas station in New York City and there
was Andy Rooney of *60 Minutes* fame, pumping his own gas.

I said, "I quote you often," and he said, "I hope with
attribution."

A few months later, I got on a plane and saw Morley Safer and
Dan Rather in first class, and then, continuing to my seat, I
saw Andy in steerage, just like me.

Another few months later, I went to a Memorial Day party in
upstate New York, where the host and hostess handed out
funny hats. When I got inside, there was Andy . . . with no
hat—drinking—next to a sign that read, "No Hat, No Drink."

Andy had wit, humility, and stubborn individuality. I admire
Andy for all these reasons, and for one more: he kept his obser-
vations short.

PUT YOUR PRESENCE
TO WORK

■   ■   ■

THE PRESENT IS all you have and you have very little
of it, just a corner of the world and time. The past you know
spottily, and the future is a vague surmise, vulnerable to flux.

Because of this, if you are more present than the average person, more awake to reality and in-the-moment, and if you can
connect the dots coming from the past to what's happening
now and extend them into the future, you have insight that is
valuable, and a chance to wake your colleagues up and get
them going in the right direction.

If this is what people mean when they talk about presence, and
if you have it (this ability to be more awake to what's happening), then you need to put your presence to work, and the best
way to do that is to speak.

ACHIEVE GREAT THINGS

■   ■   ■

PUBLIC SPEAKING IS the number one fear in America. Many of us would call it a form of *adversity*. After all, we are often required to do it against our will; it is hard to do well; and it floods us with anxiety.

Here are some thoughts on the benefits of enduring adversity.

> *"Adversity is the trial of principle. Without it, a man hardly knows whether he is honest or not."* —HENRY FIELDING

> *"If you want to know who I am, watch me when things aren't going my way."* —H. A. DORFMAN

> *"Look at the man in the midst of doubt and danger. . . . It is then that true utterances are wrung from [his] recesses. . . . The mask is torn off; the reality remains."* —LUCRETIUS

If presenting is torture for you, remember this: you will not die and you will get stronger.

PREPARATION

BE YOUR OWN BEST COACH

■　■　■

AFTER FLUBBING A GOLF SHOT, I have often called myself names. "Idiot! Dufus! Wimp!"—none of which has improved my game.

To be your own best speech coach, speak to yourself as you would to a client—be consciously positive. Over time, you'll become unconsciously positive.

As the Buddha observed, "The thought manifests as the word; the word manifests as the deed; the deed develops into habit; and habit hardens into character."

You'll improve your speaking by improving how you speak to yourself.

GATHER YOUR SELVES

■   ■   ■

WERE I TO ADD an "&" between my middle and last names, I would become Marion, Sims, & Wyeth, a tripod of a person, more stable and formidable, like a corporation.

The artist Alighiero Boetti did this in 1968 to indicate that he (and you and I) are not single, but multiple, selves. He became Alighiero e Boetti ("e" is "and" in Italian).

I have terrible stage fright, and it's probably because I have three selves. My Chicken Little self is terrified of failure and humiliation, my bulldog self believes rehearsal pays off, and my aspirational self yearns to be a spell-binding dynamo.

I get my three selves to talk to one another, so I show up sufficiently scared, well-rehearsed, and aspiring to be great, which generally gets the job done.

EXPRESS YOUR INTENTIONS CLEARLY

■ ■ ■

AS SPEAKERS WE face two big danger zones:

1. We fail to express our intentions, and
2. We express things we don't intend.

To express your intentions clearly, begin your presentation by defining what you want your audience to do and use every tool at your disposal to move them in that direction.

To avoid unintentionally expressing something, get feedback from a trusted adviser who can scrutinize your message and delivery. Speakers who begin by saying, "I'm delighted to be here . . ." while wringing their hands, swallowing loudly, and darting their eyes around the room betray their words with their body language.

Don't let your actions make liars out of your words.

OFFER QUBENS

■   ■   ■

WHEN SELLING IDEAS, products, or services, it's always good to bring up the benefits before you talk about the features. Offering qubens is better still.

Qubens are quantifiable, unique benefits, such as "Five minutes of prevention can save you five years of cure." Or "Double your order and halve your costs."

Qubens are better than vague benefits. They're specific, concrete, and measureable, and they make your presentation more persuasive.

USE METAPHORS

■　　■　　■

DURING THE DEBT CRISIS, George Shultz, the former secretary of state, made brilliantly clear what the phrase "too big to fail" means.

He reminded us that we used to have strings of lights on our Christmas trees wired in such a way that when one light went bad, all the others did too.

And then he reminded us that we had solved that problem. Now we have strings of lights on which one light can fail, while the others can keep going because each light can stand on its own.

So simple. So vivid. The power of metaphor. Use it—often!

DIG UP YOUR STORIES

■   ■   ■

SURELY YOU HAVE STORIES to tell about your own experience that will bring your message and your personality to life in high-profile moments. If you're like me, though, those stories are buried just beneath your awareness.

You can unearth them by keeping a journal; by spending a few minutes a day writing about your experiences; or by asking someone who is curious and a good listener to ask you about your life.

When you uncover stories that speak to you, they will resonate with others, and make your talks more vivid and memorable.

And P.S.: Make sure you write them down and store them in a handy place.

PRESENT THEM WITH
A PUZZLE

∎   ∎   ∎

WHAT KEEPS PEOPLE up at night? The answer is universal: open questions or unresolved problems.

When you build your presentation around an open question or an unresolved problem, you rouse the audience's primordial fascination with puzzles and problem solving. The hoopla over Y2K is a case in point: companies forked over a ton of money to solve that phantom problem.

Puzzles and problems pack a one-two punch. They trigger an emotion and then get us to think—both good ways to hold an audience.

CUT! CUT! CUT!

■   ■   ■

SPEAKING TO AN AUDIENCE is like feeding apple-
sauce to a two-year-old. The more you try to give them, the
more ends up on the floor.

Include in your text and on your slides only that information
needed to support your point.

A speech or presentation is complete when there is nothing left
to take out.

PRACTICE! PRACTICE! PRACTICE!

■　　■　　■

MY MOM AND DAD liked to say, "Old age ain't for sissies."
I say, "Neither is rehearsal."

Rehearsal can feel like going outside in your underwear. At
first, your thoughts aren't dressed in appropriate words. You
feel vulnerable. But through rehearsal, you can dress your
thoughts in formal attire or business casual, and sound like a
million bucks.

Anyway, it's better to bomb in front of colleagues in private
than in front of your audience in public. Rehearse, and where
you falter, alter.

USE THE LOCATION METHOD

■   ■   ■

WHEN WE'VE MEMORIZED a talk, we move through it *step by step:* we feel comfortable because we're *in familiar territory.* And when we can't remember, we say, *"I've lost my place,"* or "I've *misplaced* the thought."

Notice the spatial metaphors? In the classical world, when paper was scarce, speakers had to memorize their talks. And they did it by *placing* mental images of sections of a talk within images of familiar *localities.*

For instance, I might place my opening in my umbrella stand on the front porch, my first point on the rug in the front hall, and my second point in the medicine cabinet in the downstairs bathroom.

In this way, I link the content I want to memorize to what I know by heart (the layout of my home), and thereby increase the likelihood that my mind will retain, in the desired sequence, the information I mean to convey.

BUILD A LOGICAL PATTERN

▪   ▪   ▪

ORGANIZE YOUR TALK from past, to present, to future; from local, to regional, to global; from head, to heart, to hands; or from wide angle, to close up, to microscopic.

Or use perhaps the most powerful of all patterns—the *problem/ solution* model.

Define a problem confronting your audience, explore possible causes and consequences, propose your solutions, discuss alternative solutions offered by others, demonstrate their inferiority, and end with a ringing call to implement your superior idea.

MAKE YOUR IDEAS CONCRETE

■ ■ ■

BY ONE ACCOUNT, Martin Luther nailed his thoughts to the door of a church. You can nail your ideas into the memories of your listeners by using language that is vivid and concrete.

"A bird in the hand is worth two in the bush" is more memorable than, "The value of controlled assets exceeds by a factor of two those we pursue but do not yet possess."

William Carlos Williams said, "No ideas but in things." Make your ideas concrete. Play to the visual, sensory part of your audience's mind.

TELL THEM WHAT YOU'RE
NOT SAYING

■   ■   ■

EVERY WORD YOU UTTER evokes the idea of its
opposite. In other words, when you express one view, the odds
are high that your listeners will reflexively think about other,
unmentioned aspects of the topic.

For instance, if you say, "We need to commit resources to long-
term projects," mention also that you do not mean to imply
that such commitment means cutting back on investment in
current needs.

Clarify your point. Tell them what you're not saying. Speak to
create understanding, and to prevent misunderstanding.

MAKE IT LIKE A STORY

■ ■ ■

WHEN TOLD TO make your presentation like a story, you're being told to create drama because people pay attention to drama.

Drama is conflict: protagonist versus antagonist, hero versus villain. The hero can be a man (Forrest Gump), a dog (Lassie), or a fish (Nemo), and the villain, likewise, can be a man (Captain Hook), a fish (the shark in *Jaws*), or nature itself (the Perfect Storm).

In business presentations, your hero could be your product, and the villain could be the competitor whose advertising campaign is destroying your market share. Or your hero could be an entire industry, and the villain could be the prosecutorial publicity you daily receive because of the cost of your products.

Ensure that your presentation meets these requirements of any good drama:

1. The audience identifies with the hero.
2. The problems are real to the audience.
3. The stakes are high enough to mean something.

SPEAK LIKE A RIVER

∎　∎　∎

VARIETY IS THE difference between a river and a canal. A river offers a surprise around every bend—calm pools, sounding cataracts, deep gorges, spreading fields. A canal is straight and plodding.

Good presentations are like rivers, bad ones like canals. Your listeners crave variety. Engage them with broad truths buttressed by specific examples. Offer them your deep sense of purpose lightened by wit. Speak in a voice that is animated and lively. Use gestures that manifest both feeling and restraint.

Sameness is your enemy. Don't be a canal. Speak like a river.

LOGIC: THE LANGUAGE
OF PRESENTING

■   ■   ■

THE DNA OF all reasoning is the syllogism. Given A, and since B, therefore C. For instance, given all men are mortal, and since Socrates is a man, therefore Socrates is mortal.

Can you use this as the structure for a presentation? I think so. You could say: Given the situation we find ourselves in (and here you describe it in detail), and since we agree that our goals are XYZ (and here you describe your goals), therefore, this is how we move forward (and here you elaborate on your solution).

See? Logic is the language of presenting.

CHEAT AND STEAL
WHENEVER POSSIBLE

■   ■   ■

IF YOU ARE SERIOUS about getting better as a public speaker, cheat and steal whenever possible. Watch others, take what you can, and make it your own.

T. S. Eliot said, "The minor poet borrows, the great poet steals." Beethoven built on Mozart, Picasso stole from African masks, and Bob Dylan stands on the shoulders of Woody Guthrie.

The serious student of any art keeps a notebook, and in it he captures any and every random detail that excites his mind and contributes to his craft. You should do the same.

BOOST YOUR
SIGNAL-TO-NOISE RATIO

■　　■　　■

WHEN YOU LISTEN to AM radio, there's the music and there's the static. The music is the signal; the static is the noise.

All speakers have signal and noise too. A speaker's signal is the point she's trying to make, and the information and reasoning she's using to prove it.

The noise could be anything that gets in the way of the signal— too long, too detailed, too soft, too loud, no clear benefit, or an outfit that distracts the eye.

Boost the signal by sticking to your point. Kill the noise by making sure that your delivery expresses your intention.

BEGIN, BE BRIEF,
BE SEATED

■　■　■

WHY DO PEOPLE CLAP at the end of a speech?
Because it's over!

One of the great pleasures for an audience is the experience of
quickly grasping what you're getting at. They resent it if you
deprive them of this pleasure.

The correlation between the length of a talk and the value of
its content is tenuous. As Mrs. Humphrey said to her husband
Hubert when he was running for president in 1968, "Hubert,
for a speech to be immortal, it need not be interminable."

MIX THE ELEMENTS
OF SPEECH

■   ■   ■

MY COMPOST HEAP is made of leaves and grass, greens and browns, nitrogen and carbon. Mixed properly, they become a powerful, creative force yielding new life.

A good talk is a lively mix of fact and opinion, analysis and story, appeals to reason and emotion. Organized well, these elements combine to energize listeners, rouse emotion, stir new thought, and generate action.

In gardening, the mixture is called compost. In business, it's called leadership, influence, persuasion. Mix the elements of speech well, and your talks will create new life.

SAVE THE BEST FOR LAST

■   ■   ■

WHEN GIVING REASONS for a proposal, save the best reason for last. Why?

1. If you give your best reason first, the rest of the presentation peters out with trivial content.
2. If you announce that you will cover the reasons in ascending order of importance, your audience will listen more closely all the way to the end.
3. You create drama by saying, "But there's another, more important reason," after each reason you give.
4. But by far the most important reason is that when you finally get to the best reason at the end, you can set it up by saying, "But by far the most important reason is . . ."

This is showmanship, the stuff of drama. Keep the audience's interest, and end with a bang.

THE LEFT CUFF

■　■　■

THE WATCH I WEAR on my left wrist shreds the cuffs of my dress shirts. Wouldn't it be great if left cuffs were made of stronger stuff than right ones? Shirts would last longer.

If some shirtmaker did this, I would buy by the dozen because they would have solved a peculiar and nagging problem I experience. They could even make shirts for lefties with the more shred-resistant cuff on the right.

Problem definition is the key to success. Doctors know this. Speakers *should* know it. Apparently, shirtmakers don't.

ASK THE QUESTION RIGHT

■   ■   ■

IN A 1974 University of Washington study (Elizabeth Loftus and John Palmer), a group of people were asked to watch a video of a collision between two cars. Viewers who were asked, "How fast were the cars going when they smashed into each other?" gave answers averaging 40.8 mph.

But other viewers reported speeds averaging only 31.8 mph when asked, "How fast were the cars going when they made contact?" Keep in mind that each group had seen the same video only a few moments before these questions were asked.

When facilitating discussion or framing a presentation around a question, be careful how you phrase the question. Even when slightly altered, questions can generate widely different answers.

ANTICIPATORY ANXIETY

■ ■ ■

GETTING NERVOUS weeks before a speech or presentation is a good thing, because it helps you prepare. My fret
subsides when I sit down and figure out what I want to say.

Once I write it down, I have to stand up and say it aloud. I
close the door to my office, prop my papers on a music stand,
project the slides on the wall, and speak it over and over.

What I'm looking for is what actors call the *through line,* an
inner sense of the arc of the story, how it develops from scene
to scene, or in this case, slide to slide. When I have that, I'm
ready to go. I still have anxiety, but I'm chomping at the bit,
not choking at the gate.

PAY ATTENTION TO THE END

■   ■   ■

THERE'S A FLAW in my rehearsal process that causes my endings to be less effective than my openings.

I work hard on the opening, but while rehearsing, I often stop in the middle to correct something, and then start again.

In this way, the opening becomes polished but the ending suffers from neglect.

Openings and endings are equally important. Pay equal attention to both.

PROPAGATE QUESTIONS

■　　■　　■

AT BREAKFAST ONE Sunday morning, the purpose of poodles came up. We have a great standard poodle named Little Bear, but I didn't know how or why the breed came to be. Curiosity drove me to grab a laptop to fill the gap in my knowledge.

At the start of your presentation, instead of telling your audience what they need to know, ask them questions that have the potential of revealing that they lack complete knowledge of the subject you're about to address. You'll get them thinking and rouse their curiosity.

Shift your thinking from, What information do I need to convey? to What questions do I need to propagate in the mind of my audience?

P.S.: Poodles were bred to be water dogs.

YOUR WORK BECOMES
YOUR PLAY

■   ■   ■

ROBERT ZAJONC (zye-unts) spent his career as a professor of psychology at the University of Michigan, and did work that helped settle the debate over "social facilitation"—the effect of the presence of others on a person's performance of a specific task.

What Professor Zajonc found was that when performers have mastered a skill, they are helped by the presence of an audience. (Think of professional musicians or athletes.) But he also found that when performers have not yet mastered a skill, the existence of onlookers is a hindrance. (Think of Sunday duffers on the first tee.)

Beginners become masters by persisting through failure. Or as the Japanese say, "Fall down seven times, get up eight."

KNOW YOUR POINT

■ ■ ■

WHEN HIS SPEECH WRITERS handed him a script, President Eisenhower would ask, "What's the QED? Your *quod erat demonstranda*?" That's Latin for "what was demonstrated." In other words, the president was asking, At the end of your talk, what have you proven? What's your point?

Ike was testing his aides to see if they'd completed the first basic step to building a speech, which is: *Define what you want your audience to feel, think, or do.*

President Eisenhower was not a great orator in the classical sense, but he knew his classics, enough to make every speech hit its target. Hold your speech to Eisenhower's standards.

GET HEARD

■   ■   ■

I CAN HIDE the "From" field in Outlook with my hand, and tell by the "Subject" line whether a message is spam or typed by someone who knows me.

Likewise, I can close my eyes, listen to a speaker introduce her topic, and tell whether she has done her homework—and whether I'll get value from listening.

We open e-mails from people we trust, and we lend our ears to speakers who quickly demonstrate knowledge of us, interest in us, and concern for what we are concerned about.

Be one of those instantly interesting speakers.

TIE YOURSELF TO THE MAST

■   ■   ■

ULYSSES KNEW HE could not resist the Sirens, so he
developed a strategy to prevent himself from succumbing to
temptation. Before he passed their island, he tied himself to
the mast of his ship and instructed his crew not to let him
loose, no matter how desperate his pleading.

If you know your weakness as a speaker, develop a strategy to
prevent it from damaging your success. Declare a specific goal.
Tell people what you're working on. Ask them to hold you
accountable. Invite them to your presentations. Have them
sign a contract to support you, and, for you and them, let there
be consequences for failure and rewards for success.

Tie yourself to a promise and then get a little help from your
friends.

INTRODUCE YOUR WITCH

■   ■   ■

The Wizard of Oz wouldn't be much of a story—wouldn't capture and hold our attention—if it weren't for the Wicked Witch of the West. She plays an important part.

Your presentation is always more effective when there's an obstacle to overcome, a problem to fix, a myth to be busted, or a puzzle to solve.

The Wicked Witch was a problem for Dorothy, and problems bewitch companies and projects all over the world. To capture and hold attention, get your witch in the story early.

MIND YOUR DATA

■   ■   ■

The Rime of the Ancient Mariner by Samuel Taylor Coleridge includes the memorable lines: "Water, water everywhere / nor any drop to drink."

Unfortunately, many scientific and technical presentations include slide and after slide of data, data everywhere but not a thought to think.

Listeners starve on an all-data diet. Data need to be turned into *meaning,* and meaning imprinted on the mind through *story.*

In the late 90s, I had a client—a well-known AIDS doctor—who gave talks on his research. "Nobody comes to my presentations to hear the data," he said. "They come to hear what I think about the data."

Right on, Doc.

THE POWER OF HUMOR

■ ■ ■

AT THE AGE OF EIGHT, I sat in the backseat on the way to Florida enjoying the billboards for South of the Border—a gas station, truck stop, diner, and fireworks emporium tucked inside the northern border of South Carolina.

"You never sausage a place," said one, continuing, "Everyone's a wiener at South of the Border." A large hot dog hung from the sign.

Ten miles later, another appeared, "Weather report from South of the Border: Chili today. Hot tamale." I was in stitches, and begged my Dad to stop when we got there. He did.

Memories tend to cluster around emotions, positive and negative. When appropriate, pack your talk with humor. Your message is bound to be remembered.

START WITH A BANG

■   ■   ■

CAPTURE YOUR AUDIENCE'S attention from the get-go with a passionate and purposeful opening statement:

> *"Four score and seven years ago, our fathers brought forth on this continent a new nation . . ."* —PRESIDENT ABRAHAM LINCOLN

> *"When, O Catiline, do you mean to cease abusing our patience?"* —MARCUS TULLIUS CICERO

> *"I stand before you today the representative of a family in grief, in a country in mourning, before a world in shock."* —THE EARL SPENCER, BROTHER OF PRINCESS DIANA

> *"If there is anyone out there who still doubts that America is a place where all things are possible, who still wonders if the dream of our founders is alive in our time, who still questions the power of our democracy, tonight is your answer."* —PRESIDENT BARACK OBAMA

Sure beats, "Uh, I'd like to take a few minutes to say a few words about blah, blah, blah."

TELL 'EM[3]

■   ■   ■

COME TO MY HOUSE for dinner this summer. We'll have cocktails and appetizers on the front porch.

Then we'll go inside and eat a full three-course meal, and, after that, we'll sit on the back deck for coffee and dessert.

Your speeches and presentations can mimic the structure of our dinner party. Up front you feed your audience a taste of what you're going to say. Then you serve them the meat of the matter, and you end with a sweet reminder of what you've said.

Think of it as tell 'em[3]: Tell 'em what you're gonna tell 'em, tell 'em, and then tell 'em what you told 'em.

It's a simple way to structure a presentation, not all that dramatic, but useful in a pinch.

BORING IN
TEN SECONDS FLAT

■   ■   ■

A FAMOUS PREACHER in England was invited to preach before Queen Victoria, and he was warned that Her Majesty preferred her sermons short.

At the end of his sermon, the queen said to him, "Sir, you were brief." He said, "Ah, Ma'am, I like never to be tedious." She said, "You were also tedious."

Surprise! You can be boring in ten seconds flat. To avoid being boring, start with a story that creates dramatic tension, approach a familiar issue from an unusual perspective, or do or say something unpredictable.

Predictability kills interest from the start.

IS CONTENT KING?

■   ■   ■

"What you are speaks so loudly that no one can hear what you're saying." —RALPH WALDO EMERSON

If you are reading this book, you are a content-oriented individual, committed to the power of proof and reasoning. If you can prove something is true, you probably assume others will feel compelled to accept it.

Good content is often necessary for persuasion, but usually not sufficient. The landscape of history is littered with content-rich arguments that went nowhere.

The rational mind is the tip of the iceberg. The rest of the mind goes deeper than that. Your content may be king, but your character and motivation count too.

Look in the mirror or go to the videotape. Consider your manner and motives.

THE UNEXPECTED

■   ■   ■

WATCHING OBAMA'S INAUGURATION in 2008, I perked up like a bird dog when Chief Justice Roberts flubbed the oath. The moment demonstrated the attention-getting and memory-creating power of . . . the unexpected.

Can you discover something unexpected to say or do when presenting? Can you use a prop? Do something unusual? Say something surprising or controversial?

The unexpected wakes an audience up, and six days, six weeks, six months later, they remember the moment when you took them by surprise.

TRY THE THREE WHYS

■   ■   ■

A FEW YEARS AGO, I had a client in private equity who liked to begin his fund-raising pitch to investors new to the asset class with, "I think there are three questions on the table: Why private equity? Why private equity in emerging markets? And why us?"

It's a practical approach, simple and business-like. It puts the listener at ease, and offers him the prospect of an education without making him feel pressured or uninformed.

Use the three whys to provide the skeletal structure for a simple argument. And remember, telling stories and including a *why not* or two will add to your credibility. No investment is perfect.

ELECTRIFY THEM

■　　■　　■

My words fly up, my thoughts remain below.
Words without thoughts never to heaven go.

So says Claudius in Shakespeare's *Hamlet*, and he's not the only one whose lack of thought when speaking has caused his words to fall flat.

The electricity of thought lights up speech. Reading or reciting a text can short-circuit that power and turn a brilliantly written speech into something lifeless.

The answer? Rehearse aloud enough to familiarize yourself with the ideas and intentions beneath the words. Keep your eyes on your audience, especially at the ends of your sentences. And improvise now and then, so at least some of your words are more charged with the energy of thinking.

GET OUT OF YOUR BOTTLE

■   ■   ■

"IT'S HARD TO READ the label when you're inside the bottle." Meaning: it is hard to see yourself the way others see you.

As I've written elsewhere, you intend things that you don't express and you express things that you don't intend. We all have blind spots.

Videotaping yourself during rehearsal can help. But you should also get feedback from friends, spouses, mentors, and clients to fine-tune how you show up in the world.

Half of what you hear will make you feel good. The rest will sting . . . and make you a better speaker.

SPILL THE BEANS
IN REHEARSAL

■ ■ ■

EINSTEIN WROTE THAT he discovered the theory of
relativity by imagining he was riding on a lightning bolt. Sustained visualization led him to breakthrough thinking.

Sustained *verbalization*—stream-of-consciousness talking—can
lead to similar outcomes. In rehearsal, allowing yourself to say
anything that comes to mind brings fleeting thoughts and new
ideas into the light of your conscious awareness.

We know more than we can say, and we can say more than we
can write. Spill the beans in rehearsal.

PROTECT YOURSELF FROM
UNWANTED QUESTIONS

■　　■　　■

IF YOU DON'T want to talk about it, or answer questions
about it, don't mention it in the course of your talk or put it on
a slide.

Certain people in the audience notice small details and ask
penetrating questions. Others lob random questions to probe
for weaknesses in your methods, facts, or knowledge.

If it complicates your point, if it's not essential for your argument, if there's no ethical reason why the audience should
know it, then by all means leave it out.

BE DECOROUS

■ ■ ■

KENNETH BURKE, in his book *A Rhetoric of Motives* (1950), argued for the importance of *decorum* when speaking to groups. Every audience and circumstance is different, so a speaker must adjust to the expectations of the moment.

> You persuade a man only insofar as you talk his language
> by speech, gesture, tonality, order, image [and] attitude.

In other words, don't quote Shakespeare at half-time in the locker room, and don't use your four-lettered Anglo-Saxonisms in the boardroom. Suit yourself to the occasion.

SPEND MORE TIME
ON THE PROBLEM

■   ■   ■

THE DECLARATION OF INDEPENDENCE lists twenty-six injuries the British monarchy inflicted on the American colonists. The injuries, listed together, read like a ticking bomb, and comprise nearly half the text. They create the rationale for change and the emotion needed to make that change.

When you want to speak persuasively, spend time on the problem. Be fair and accurate in your descriptions of the facts, causes, and consequences, but go ahead and pile them up, one after the other, so they reach a critical mass, enough to be convincing.

In business, we sometimes soft-pedal the problem we seek to solve so we don't appear negative or to avoid stepping on toes. Understandable. But there are times when it's right to lay all the issues on the table, one by one, to beat the drum for revolution.

CAPTURE AND KEEP
ATTENTION

■ ■ ■

EVERY YEAR IN the United States we create 60,000 new books, 18,000 magazines, 20 billion pages of editorial content on food and nutrition alone, 400,000 scholarly journals, 15 billion catalogues, and 87.2 billion pieces of direct mail.

Herbert Simon, a Nobel Prize–winning economist, spoke about the relationship between information and attention. He said, "What information consumes is rather obvious: it consumes the attention of its recipients. Hence a wealth of information creates a poverty of attention."

In the age of big data, unlike any age before, the problem is not lack of information. The problem is collecting it, organizing it, analyzing it, and taking action on it.

Your challenge as a speaker in this brave new world is to so effectively crunch and interpret the data that you not only capture and keep attention for the time it takes to get your point across, but you also convince your audience to take wise, considered action.

DO THE MATH

∎ ∎ ∎

MOST FORMAL SALES presentations follow this blueprint:

1. Who we are
2. What we do
3. How we do it
4. Why we're cool
5. A few more facts about us
6. Yup, it's still about us
7. Go ahead, ask us questions about us

But Adecco, a global leader in temporary staffing, has built a different, highly effective model for their sales presentations.

At Adecco they like to say, "In sales-call math, 3 + 4 does not equal 4 + 3." In other words, a good sales presentation first demonstrates an understanding of at least three things about the prospect (their drivers, objectives, and problems/opportunities) before it launches into "Who we are, What we do, Why we're different, and Where we've done it before," four things all about the seller.

Talk about them first. It adds value to the talk about yourself.

GIVE YOUR TALK A SPINE

AUDIENCES DISLIKE INVERTEBRATE presentations. They like talks, and presenters, with spines.

Don't assume that because you have an agenda slide you have a vertebrate talk. An agenda can be a random list of topics—a knee bone connecting to a head bone. Audiences like a story-like structure in which each slide fits logically into the next.

And while we're on the subject of spines, stand up for your ideas. Out of the clash of many minds come the best results.

THE OTHER SIDE OF COMPLEXITY

■   ■   ■

"I DON'T GIVE a hoot for simplicity this side of complexity, but I'd give the world for it on the other side."

This remark has been attributed to Einstein, Shaw, Twain, Churchill, and Wilde—the usual suspects for insight packed tightly into wit.

Whoever said it, it makes sense for speakers. Listeners appreciate a speaker who can clarify complexity, without oversimplifying it.

AVOID THE FALSE CHOICE

■   ■   ■

WHEN GIVING A presentation to an executive committee, which do you think is worse: a presentation exhaustingly
long and detailed but accurate and complete, or one that is
brief and accessible but lacks detail?

In my experience, less experienced speakers think the brief and
accessible choice is worse. They fear it could make them look
unprepared: they want to have everything on the slides.

In most cases, this is a false choice. If a message isn't easily
understood as the basis for making a decision or prediction, it's
not much use to an executive committee.

FOCUS ON YOUR AUDIENCE

■   ■   ■

WE ALL GET ANNOYED when doctors, lawyers, and accountants speak their special lingos. Only the rare ones bother to translate their advice into plain English.

Yet here's the paradox. The less they use their special lingo, the more we respect them for their expertise.

Speak to your audience in the language of your audience, about what is most important to your audience.

DELIVERY

DON'T HIDE. SIMPLY CONNECT.

■ ■ ■

PUBLIC SPEAKING IS frightening for most of us. Some of us hide behind a mountain of polished content, scripted out word for word, dismissing as mere showmanship the ability to engage an audience.

Others, more rare, try to dazzle with a performance, ratcheting up their voice and gestures in an effort to mask their fear.

Both approaches sidestep the essential task of speaking, which is to simply connect with an audience on an equal level.

Be prepared. Be real. Have enough energy to hold attention, and look them in the eyes. You want to be heard, and they want to know that you *get* them.

FOCUS ON YOUR FOCUS

■   ■   ■

STAGE FRIGHT IS a strange thing. It seems to come when we fixate on the possible problem rather than on the goal we want to achieve or the process we're using to reach the goal.

In tennis, we don't look at the net. In golf, we don't look at the sand trap. We look at the ball, and at the target.

Focus on getting focused on the right thing. Focus either on the outcome you want, or on the process you're using to get it.

LOOK AT YOUR LISTENERS

■ ■ ■

Q: When you look at your listeners, one at a time, where are they likely to look?

A: At me.

Q: Good. And if you don't look at your listeners when you're speaking to them, where won't they look?

A: They won't look at me?

Q: Right. They'll look at you less. And where will they look when they're looking away?

A: Somewhere else?

Q: Probably. And when they're looking somewhere else, what are they thinking about?

A: Something else.

Q: Correct. So where should you look when speaking to your listeners?

A: I should look at them.

Q: Good. Shall we practice?

SHY GUYS CAN PRESENT

■   ■   ■

SHY PRESENTERS ARE appealing to me because I see them as vulnerable and authentic. Also, like a British accent, shyness can boost a shy guy's perceived intelligence quotient. For me, the shy have great credibility.

However, if a shy guy makes me worry he's going to have a meltdown, or he speaks so quietly that I have trouble hearing him, or he cowers like a mouse, or he's just plain boring because he refuses to actually SHOW UP as a personality, then I get frustrated with him and tune out.

The best strategy for a shy presenter is to be concise, well-rehearsed, clever with words, and humorous now and then. Forget theatrics. That's a language the shy should not dare to speak.

CONSIDER YOUR VOICE
THE THUNDER

■　　■　　■

LYING IN BED as a child, I would watch a bolt of lightning flood the space of my room, and then count the seconds to the clap of thunder. Five Mississippis meant the storm was a mile away.

Lightning comes before thunder. Similarly, when you rise to give a talk, your image precedes your sound. As you walk to the front of the room, you flash across the vision of your listeners, creating a first impression.

But you haven't spoken yet, haven't made a sound. So wait a few seconds before you begin. Count to five, and then begin your talk.

Your voice will be the thunder.

FLIP YOUR SWITCH

■   ■   ■

IN 1960 MARILYN MONROE took a taxi with a friend. The cab driver looked in the rearview mirror and said to Marilyn, "Hey, lady, if ya lost a few pounds and put on some lipstick, you could pass for Marilyn Monroe."

Marilyn looked at her friend. "Should I?" she asked. "Why not?" said her friend. So Marilyn flipped some inner switch, and at once she was the Hollywood Marilyn, the one who could light up a room.

If you have a switch, flip it!

BE BRIEF, NOT TERSE

■   ■   ■

CALVIN COOLIDGE, the thirtieth president of the United States, was called "Silent Cal" because he was truly a man of few words.

Once, after the president had attended church, a reporter asked him, "What was the sermon about, Mr. President?"

"Sin," answered Coolidge.

"What did he say about it?"

"He was against it."

Depending on the president's facial expression, such brevity could have communicated unfriendliness or bone-dry humor.

Another story: A woman in a receiving line at the White House gushed to him, "Mr. President, I bet my husband that I could get you to say more than two words."

"You lose," was Coolidge's reply.

Terseness is a kind of hostility. Brevity, on the other hand, implies clarity without elaboration.

Be brief, not terse.

ASSERT YOURSELF

■ ■ ■

AMY CUDDY is an associate professor at Harvard Business School. She has done research indicating that holding an assertive body posture for two minutes can increase your level of testosterone, the confidence hormone, regardless of your sex.

The research also demonstrates that holding a timid or submissive posture for the same time increases your level of cortisol, the anxiety hormone.

If you suffer from stage fright, if you're insecure, if you're conflict averse, Professor Cuddy's data offers you hope. You can change the way you feel and the way you're perceived when you adopt assertive behaviors.

LOOK, YOU. DON'T POINT!

■　■　■

A FEW YEARS AGO I was playing back a video of a presentation my client, a Texan, had delivered to his corporate board. I paused the camcorder to show him that he was pointing to his slides with his middle finger.

"Oh my God!" he drawled, "I'm flippin' the chairman the bird!"

When on stage, it's a good idea to point with your whole hand rather than use a single finger. It looks better, more assertive. The first finger alone is accusative, the pinky is prissy, the ring finger spastic, and the middle one is downright hostile.

Point with your whole hand.

CHOOSE YOUR VOICE

■ ■ ■

IF YOU HAVE TO CHOOSE what to work on—your voice or your body language—choose your voice.

Your voice expresses logic *and* feeling. Your body language only gets noticed if it's crummy.

Your voice also has more influence over your gestures than vice versa. Think about it: music has more influence over dancers than dancers have over music. Have you ever seen a performance in which dancers move and musicians respond to their movements? I haven't. Sound controls movement, movement does not control sound.

Yes, you need both: a lively voice and appropriate body language. But in business, the only body language you need is the look of comfort and authority.

MAKE THE MOST
OF YOUR WORST

■   ■   ■

I HAD A CLIENT from India who spoke with a pro-
nounced Indian accent. He had a standard opening line.

Standing at the lectern, he would look out at the audience and
say, with a smile on his face, "Hello, my name is Deepak. As
you can tell from my accent, I am from Cleveland."

Robert Reich, Clinton's very short secretary of labor, once
began a talk this way: "When I began to worry about the political economy of the United States, I was six foot four . . . It
wore me down."

Both used self-effacing humor, the best kind. From these openings on, the audience listened, delighted by the humor and
eager to connect with men who had the self-awareness to
acknowledge what the audience could have seen as limitations.
Go ahead. Make the most of your worst.

DRESS FOR SUCCESS

■   ■   ■

ALL COMMUNICATION HAS substance, structure, and surface. One surface is your clothing.

For professional occasions, dress conservatively, which means be stylish but not fashionable. Fashion is often out of style, but style is never out of fashion.

Men, it's generally a good idea to wear a suit or a sport jacket to hide your belly and the wrinkles in your pants. Also, a red tie captures the eye.

Ladies, wear closed-toe shoes with medium heels, nude or dark hosiery, a jacket, and a bit of red near the face. Lipstick, a red scarf, or a red suit will get the job done.

At a glance, your clothes should announce, "Professional," so that all attention is on what you say, not what you wear.

BE THE TREE

■ ■ ■

LEARN TO STAND STILL as a presenter. Be the still
point in the turning world. Get your weight on both feet.
Don't stick one hip out like a pop singer. Instead, be the tree.

Stand as if you guard something sacred. Stand as if you stand
for something. When you change your subject, move, and
then stand still again. The juxtaposition of stillness with movement is very near the crux of any performance art.

LEARN TO PAUSE

■   ■   ■

THE ABILITY TO PAUSE effectively lends you stature and helps listeners listen. Here is an exercise I learned from Marian Rich, a legendary voice and speech teacher in New York City, who was a mentor to my wife and me.

The exercise is simply that—an exercise—designed to help you bring language to life.

Mark a paragraph / in this manner / into the shortest possible phrases. / First, / whisper it / with energetic lips / breathing / at all the breath marks. /

Then / speak it / in the same way. / Do this / with a different paragraph / every day. / Keep your hand / on your abdomen / to make sure / that it moves out / when you breathe in / and moves in / when you speak.

The exercise will help you frame your phrases with a sliver of silence.

IGNITE THEIR INTEREST

■   ■   ■

SMOKERS LIKE MATCHES that light with the first strike, and listeners like presentations that ignite their interest immediately.

Avoid such stutter steps as, "I'd like to take a few minutes to talk a little bit about . . ." Start with the pitch; don't start with the windup.

Look one person in the eye as you deliver your opening. "It looks like there's a storm brewing in the ketchup market," you say as you begin. And a hundred pairs of eyes open a little wider.

MAKE IT A DIALOGUE

■　　■　　■

WHEN YOU THROW a dart at a dartboard, you watch to see where it lands. When speaking to an audience, do the same thing: watch your listeners to see how they respond.

Do this and your speech approximates dialogue. You say what you think, read their reactions, and respond by adjusting your tone, asking a question, or ploughing ahead when you see heads nod.

"Presentation," in many quarters, is a dirty word. But "conversation" carries no such baggage. Make your presentations conversations.

STAY AHEAD OF YOUR TOES

■   ■   ■

IF WHILE SPEAKING you are struck dead by lightning, listeners would like you to fall forward.

They like strong speakers, forward leaning and forward looking, speakers who speak as if on the balls of their feet, balanced, moving toward an objective.

They dislike flat-footed speakers, speakers who seem to be plodding, pedestrian, not very exciting.

And God forbid you get back on your heels so when lightning strikes you fall backward. Back-pedaling is defensive, and makes you look like you're on the run.

Good speaker footwork is when your head, heart, and hands stay ahead of your toes.

GLOTTAL FRY

■   ■   ■

GRINDING YOUR VOICE is not attractive. Emily Post would look over the top of her glasses at you, like Judge Judy, if she caught you at it.

Yet I have noticed on radio, TV, and in my own practice that many young people are speaking with a glottal fry.

What is it? If you imitate Elmer Fudd saying, "Be vewy vewy quiet. I'm hunting wabbits," you will be using glottal fry.

It's a vocal mannerism that grinds the vocal chords, producing a gravelly, grinding sound, as if the speaker had run out of air. I associate it with laziness, immaturity, and intimacy in private places.

The cure is simple: open your mouth and throat, and support your voice with a good, strong breath. Don't fry your words like bacon bubbling in fat.

BE PITCH PERFECT

■   ■   ■

IN WELL-SPOKEN ENGLISH, there is a change of pitch on every stressed syllable. Let's try that again. In **well-spoken English**, there is a **change** of **pitch** on **eve**ry **stressed syll**able.

Vocal emphasis brings your meaning to life. Not everything is equally important. Don't be a Johnny One-Note. Expressiveness is a significant part of effectiveness.

Vary the pitch of your speaking voice.

VISIBLY ENJOY YOUR
BELIEFS

■　　■　　■

W. B. YEATS was arguably the greatest English-language poet of the twentieth century. He once made the following observation:

> I always think a great speaker convinces us not by force of reasoning but because he is visibly enjoying the beliefs he wants us to accept.

In other words, emotions are contagious. Make sure yours are worth catching.

LET *THEM* CLAP

■   ■   ■

"ALRIGHTY, THEN!" you say, and clap your hands
repeatedly as you stand to bring the room to order.

In formal settings, listeners can bristle when a speaker claps at
the start. It can be seen as abrupt and inappropriate, as if you
were treating the audience like schoolchildren.

Earn their attention some other way—by being still and silent,
or by moving among them to quiet them down.

Don't clap at the start. Let *them* do the clapping when you're
done.

MIND THE GAPS

■　　■　　■

I ONCE SPENT a day with a brilliant man who managed to wedge into the gaps between words handfuls of "Okays?" and "You knows." Instead of listening to his content, I counted "Okays." (I am sure you have all done this.)

Eventually I gave up counting and began to think about dinner.

The spaces between words are as important to your message as the words themselves. We need white space between written words and little gaps of silence between spoken ones.

Preserve the silences that make speech more effective.

STRIVE FOR
THE GOLDEN MEAN

■　　■　　■

WHEN THREATENED, a possum contracts into a ball of submission, while a bear stands on her hind legs to make herself look dominant.

When you feel threatened as a speaker try to avoid both extremes. If you contract, your ability to inspire confidence diminishes. On the other hand, overdoing it is no good either. Audiences don't like to be dominated.

Strive for the golden mean: high energy, low tension, and a relationship with the audience that is based on equality—not dominance or submission.

DON'T BE A SCHOOLMARM

■   ■   ■

WHEN AN AUDIENCE is unresponsive to your hearty, "Good morning, everyone!" please avoid the temptation to say in an even louder and more enthusiastic voice, "Let's try that again. *Good morning, everyone!*"

While such an approach might serve teachers who have positional authority over kids, it won't work for you because you have to earn authority with adult audiences.

Rather than correcting your audience for their indifferent response, take responsibility for their experience. It's not their job to be interested. It's your job to get them interested.

STEP IT UP A NOTCH

■   ■   ■

THE GREEK GENERAL Xenophon, who was in charge of keeping the Persians at bay, knew how to get his army to fight.

In one battle, he positioned his troops at the top of a hill with a cliff dropping steeply behind them. Their only chance of survival was forward, into the enemy.

Can you do this for yourself, to take your skills to another level? Take on an assignment that scares you to death? Leave the script and the PowerPoint behind? Get away from the lectern, the normal and predictable?

Step into your fear, into the moment, and move out into the audience.

DON'T ZIP YOUR SPEECH

■ ■ ■

HERE'S HOW SOME people talk: they begin their statements in a normal way, and then they *suddenlyracetotheend*.

If they were to drive the same way they talk, it would be horrible to be a passenger in their car. Your neck would frequently snap back *likeadummyinacarcrash*.

In these bursts of speed, all consonants are elided, the mouth barely moves, and *yougottaguesswhattheysaid*.

If this is you, please don't talk like a Zip file. Every letter in every word is a code for a position of the tongue and the other organs of speech. Be present in that analog movement.

TURN THE PAGE IN SILENCE

■ ■ ■

LESS IS MORE. People can only retain three to five points. And studies indicate that attention drops off after twenty minutes.

So, if you have to give a long talk, break it into twenty-minute chunks and give the audience a breather. Or just stop talking for a few seconds as you leave one section and begin the next.

Symphonies have movements, and the arresting silences between them.

SKIN THE CAT YOUR WAY

■   ■   ■

I HEARD TWO TALKS at a memorial service, each distinguished for different reasons.

In the first, the speaker stepped to the lectern and said, "On a summer afternoon in 1986, an old gray Peugeot pulled into the driveway belching white smoke. The door opened and out stepped Tommy." It was formal and vivid.

In the second, the speaker smiled, looked at the audience, and said quietly, "Wow, this is a huge crowd." His tone and demeanor were disarmingly authentic and relaxed. He was informal and his character spoke volumes.

Two ways to skin the cat. Both good.

MIND YOUR Ps AND Qs

■ ■ ■

THE THEATER AT Epidaurus is considered to have the finest acoustics of any ancient theater in Greece. For centuries, no one knew why. Now scientists think they have the answer.

Grooves in the backrests of the stone seats dampen the low frequencies and amplify the high. In speech, vowels are the low frequencies. The high frequencies are consonants, which are harder to project.

Few of the rooms in which you speak will have the acoustics of Epidaurus. If you want to be heard, mind your Ps and Qs— and all their fellow consonants.

BE THE HUNTER

■   ■   ■

EAGLES HAVE EYES that face forward. They're hunters. They have binocular vision, which gives them depth perception. They're near the top of the food chain.

Rabbits have eyes on the sides of their head. They're hunted. They have low binocularity. They twitch their heads back and forth, watching out for danger. Rabbits are hunted by eagles, hunted and eaten for breakfast.

You have eyes on the front of your head. You're a hunter. You hunt for nods, smiles, leanings in, and shouts of approval. You're the top of the food chain. Don't be the hunted. Be the hunter. Focus your eyes on your listeners, one at a time.

WATCH YOUR TONE

■   ■   ■

READY FOR A BIG WORD? Paralinguistics! It's your vocal image—all those things you do with words when you speak: fast talk, up-talk, monotony, repetitive pitch patterns, breathiness, throatiness—all those qualities of sound that get interpreted by your audience and go into the impression you create.

In his book *Blink*, Malcolm Gladwell reported that the insurance industry discovered that surgeons who get sued have one thing in common: a gruff tone of voice. People who feel wronged (even if there was no medical error) are more likely to sue a surgeon who was gruff than one whose tone was empathetic.

Tone of voice counts. Style has substance. Watch your paralinguistics, buster!

AVOID SQUIRREL PAWS

■　■　■

MY GRANDMOTHER used to take me to the Central Park Zoo in New York to feed peanuts to squirrels.

The squirrels were tame, and stood on their hind legs begging with their front paws hanging in front of their chests.

I see speakers with squirrel paws—limp-wristed hands devoid of life—and no matter how bright the speaker, I am not impressed.

A squirrel-paw speaker doesn't look like a person who can get anything done. Pump energy and life into your hands to demonstrate your bias for action.

WATCH YOUR MOUTH

■ ■ ■

I SAW TWO PEOPLE whose mouths did weird things when they listened.

One pushed her lips over to one side of her face. She looked like a Picasso painting.

The other pulled a corner of his mouth back toward his ear. He looked like a mother hen clucking in disapproval.

A neutral-to-open face, eyes focused on the speaker, eyebrows slightly raised in an expression of interest, mouth in a tiny smile, head nodding (with a slight cocking of an ear) would be more encouraging of a healthy dialogue.

DON'T FORGET YOUR HANDS

■　■　■

GESTURE IS NOT mere decoration: rather, it is the yang that completes the yin of spoken words.

When Professor William McNeil tied the hands of speakers behind their backs, the speakers took longer than usual to find the right words.

In other experiments he found that listeners lose much of the meaning when a speaker's hands are not engaged in talking.

Gestures are another vocabulary, other than speech, that speak to the brain through the eyes. Let your hands be part of your message.

HIDE THE ART

. . .

BALDASSARE CASTIGLIONE WAS a courtier who wrote *The Book of the Courtier*, a global best-seller in the mid-sixteenth century.

In it he urges us "in all things to practice a certain nonchalance which conceals all artistry and makes whatever one says or does seem uncontrived and effortless."

In fact, he reports that many ancient orators feigned a kind of plainspoken folksiness, "for if the people had known of their skills, they would have been frightened of being deceived."

In other words, the art of effective public speaking lies in hiding the art.

BE A LION TAMER

■　■　■

SPEAKING TO A CROWD of any size can feel like lion taming: a dangerous occupation due to the obvious risks of toying with powerful instinctive carnivores.

To show them who's boss, look them in the eye one at a time. Throw them a compliment once in a while. Poke them with a question now and then to feed their egos. Strut in front of them like you were born to crack the whip.

It's an act requiring deep knowledge of the audience. You can't show fear, or they'll eat you alive. Take charge. Be a lion tamer.

GIVE IN ORDER TO GET

■   ■   ■

MY DOG IS often reluctant to give me his toy so I can throw it and he can have the wild pleasure of going to get it. I have to assume he's not familiar with the idea of giving in order to get.

Lucky for us speakers, we know that the more we give of ourselves—in terms of preparation, authenticity, and self-disclosure—the more we'll get in return from our listeners.

Don't play "keep away" with your audience. Put yourself deeply into the challenge of speaking. Use personal stories to show them who you are. Doing so is one of the great satisfactions of speaking, and of listening.

SHOW YOUR FACE

■   ■   ■

WHEN PRESENTING, fix your hair so the audience can see your whole face.

You are simply more present—more *in the room*—if they can see your eyes and forehead. Your forehead is like a billboard on Times Square: your eyebrows speak volumes, as do your eyes. Use them to your advantage.

Keep hair away from your cheeks and mouth. When you turn sideways toward a visual, your profile should not be obscured by a shock of hair.

Bangs cast a shadow and a closed curtain of hair hides the most important real estate on stage: your face.

PRAY FOR AN AUDIENCE
WITH LOW EXPECTATIONS

■ ■ ■

ASKED TO DEFINE the best quality in a spouse, Warren Buffet replied, "Low expectations."

That's a good quality in an audience too. When they expect something long, dry, and predictable and you come out with something crisp, lively and engaging, you get a boost in your approval rating.

On the other hand, if they expect you to walk on water and you swim like a mere mortal, you're sunk.

Pray for an audience with low expectations.

ON THE PODIUM, LEAN DOWNHILL

■ ■ ■

AT SNOWBIRD IN UTAH, a friend led me to a slope so steep I didn't dare lean downhill, which is exactly what I should have done. Instead, I leaned back in fear, fell hard, and slid headfirst to the bottom.

My belief that I couldn't handle the situation made me fearful and tentative. I argued for my limitations, and I got to keep them.

As a speaker, when you get to the front of the room, don't change your plans. Stay committed to your message. Don't be tentative. Lean downhill.

NARROW YOUR FOCUS

■   ■   ■

TOLD THAT HIS OPPONENT knew his weakness and had a plan to knock him out, Mike Tyson replied, "Everyone has a plan . . . until they get hit."

This holds true for speakers as for boxers. Five hundred squinty-eyed faces can knock the stuffing out of you.

Great performers narrow their focus. They put aside fear and thoughts of success and bear down to get the job done.

DESIGN AND USE OF VISUAL AIDS

MEMORIZE YOUR OPENING

■　■　■

MEMORIZE YOUR OPENING and deliver it while the title slide is on the screen. The lack of detail on the title slide allows the audience to focus entirely on you.

This increased focus creates a pivotal moment—an opportunity to connect with the audience, demonstrate your grasp of the subject, establish the importance of your theme, and preview your main ideas.

Memorize your opening because it's the part of your talk your audience is most likely to remember.

MANAGE TECHNOLOGY'S
SIDE EFFECTS

■   ■   ■

A/V TECHNOLOGIES ARE like drugs: they all have side effects. You have to learn to manage them.

Teleprompters make you sound like you're reading. Power-Point splits your attention between your slides and your audience. Microphones make you think you can lower your degree of intention, which drains the electricity out of your voice.

Technology is helpful, but there is no substitute for connecting with your listeners, knowing your lines, and speaking with just the right *oomph*.

AVOID USING BULLETS

■   ■   ■

SPEAKERS WHO READ bullet points are targets for criticism. After all, why hold a meeting and merely read aloud what your listeners could have read at their desks?

To keep your reputation out of the crosshairs, make your bullets short so they simply trigger your thoughts about a given subject. If you're worried that you'll forget your lines because your bullets are too short, rehearse more.

And if you're loading your slides with bullets because you fear they won't be clear to those who should be at your meeting but can't attend, put the details into an appendix or in the notes section of PowerPoint, rather than cramming them onto slides.

TURN OFF THE PROJECTOR

■　　■　　■

TURN OFF THE PROJECTOR now and then. Turn off the light and the hum of the fan, the white noise and the rectangular slab of glare. Turn off the headline and the text.

Step away from the corner of the room and stand up, front and center. Talk to your audience. Just talk for a while, the old-fashioned way, without slides. Push the "B for Black" button on your computer and see what happens.

The room will morph from predictably corporate to surprisingly intimate, and in that moment, you gain access to the personal space of your listeners.

Turn off the projector. You are the most important visual.

BE THE LOCOMOTIVE

■   ■   ■

AS THE SPEAKER, you are the locomotive that pulls the train of thought. Your strength of purpose keeps you and your audience on track.

This means that transitions from slide to slide are moments at which you, the speaker, must quickly focus the attention of the listener.

For instance, with the current slide up, you might say, "Now that we've established an unmet medical need in the asthma market, let's look at our competition."

Only then should you advance to the next slide, when you've pointed your listeners in the right direction. This helps them round the corner from one topic to the next as your argument builds up steam.

STATE YOUR CLAIM

■   ■   ■

THE HEADLINE of a slide, like a billboard, should make a claim, and the words, pictures, or graphs in the body of the slide should prove the claim made in the headline.

"We can go to market in a year" would be a better headline for a slide than "Time to Market" because it makes a claim. Under the headline, a timeline with key milestones on it would be one way to suggest that the claim is valid.

"We face massive generic intrusion," would be a better headline for a pharmaceutical marketer's slide than "Market Outlook" because it expresses a point of view and is brimming with intellectual and emotional *content*.

Don't use slide headlines to introduce a topic. Use them to make a statement.

DO NOT USE OTHER PEOPLE'S SLIDES

■   ■   ■

OTHER PEOPLE'S SLIDES are like other people's clothes: they don't fit and they make you look bad.

Your own slides follow your own logic and experience, which are the sources of your passion and credibility.

When asked to use other people's slides, insist on your right to make them your own. Don't go to the party in hand-me-downs.

BEAT THE BUSY SLIDE

■   ■   ■

IF YOU ARE FORCED to use a busy slide, you can overcome its pernicious tendency to put your audience into a daze by being both vocally and physically assertive.

Say, for example, "Please look at line 36 of this chart," and then stride over to the screen and point like Ahab sighting Moby Dick's head, surfacing. Or, "Here you see that the Oshkosh region outperformed all others. Why is that?" and then move forward to answer your own question.

In other words, be highly directive, like a Roman traffic cop I saw one summer, whose hands in white gloves expressed such Jovian authority that contending streams of traffic obeyed him meekly.

SPECIAL
OCCASIONS

CONQUER THE ENEMIES
OF SALES

■ ■ ■

THE ENEMY OF SPEED on a bike is friction—
resistance from road and air. The massive growth in bike
technology has reduced friction, ounce by ounce, and
increased speed, second by second.

The enemy of success in sales presenting is also friction—
resistance from prejudice, skepticism, and inertia. Going after
new business, cold-calling, and e-mail marketing can be a long
slog up a steep hill. Tiny reductions in friction can lead to
significant results.

To conquer prejudice, become familiar. To overcome skepticism, prove your points. And to prod inertia, arouse in your
audience an eager want or take them by surprise and challenge
their thinking.

BE A GOOD PANELIST

■　　■　　■

IF YOU ARE ASKED to be a conference panelist, keep this list at hand:

1. Prep. Then go with the flow.
2. Be brief. Short is better. Don't be a bore.
3. Be specific. Lofty is lovely, but not from a panelist. Keep it concrete.
4. Be provocative. Disagree agreeably. Do it often, not always.
5. Smile. Show your teeth. You're never fully dressed without your teeth showing.
6. Get heard. Speak loud. Make your mic work. Sound systems generally suck.
7. Talk to someone, panelist, moderator, or audience member. The audience wants to hear you engage in lively conversation.
8. Don't wait. Jump in early and often. Mix it up.
9. Bury your pride. Don't whine if you get intellectually mugged. It's good for the panel, entertaining for the audience, and probably good for you.
10. Have fun. Right there. Right then. Light up the room.

Adapted from Paul Kedrosky, paul.kedrosky.com/blog.

BE A GOOD PANEL MODERATOR

■   ■   ■

MOST PANELS ARE boring—talking heads sitting at a table. But when you get to be a panel moderator, you can liven it up by using these ten techniques:

1. Be quiet. Listen. Ignite the conversation and let it burn.
2. Be loud. Be big. Be the boss. Inspire confidence.
3. Be prepared. Know the subject. Steer the discussion. Have questions, quotes, and obscure Dylan lyrics at the ready.
4. Be an invisible conductor. Play your panelists like musical instruments. Bring out the best in each of them.
5. Be able to think about more than two things at once: the current discussion, your overall plan, the time, where you want to go next.
6. Be deferential. You're not the star. The panelists are.
7. Be ruthless, the audience's advocate—on time, answers, and issues.
8. Be clear. Ask short questions and make clear statements.

9. Be timely. Start on time, keep it moving, and end on time. Ostentatiously check your watch.
10. Be fun. Not funereal, unsmiling, and ponderous, or all three at once.

Adapted from Paul Kedrosky, paul.kedrosky.com/blog.

HIT 'EM WITH A ZINGER

■   ■   ■

WHEN YOU'RE SEATED at a conference table listening to the conversation, and you decide you need to say something, say it well.

Sum up what you have to say in a zinger, like, "Continuous improvement is better than postponed perfection. Let's launch and learn." Then state one, and only one, reason for this bold assertion.

"When Jobs and Gates launched their first products, those products were bug-ridden vaporware. Consumers stuck with them through every iteration, and made them better. They'll do the same with us."

To wrap it up, repeat your zinger: "Continuous improvement is better than postponed perfection. Let's launch and learn."

Bingo. Done. Well said.

THE ROLE OF MR. INSIDE

■　　■　　■

IN EVERY BUSINESS, there's a Mr. Inside and a Mrs.
Outside. Mrs. Outside brings in the business, and Mr. Inside
runs the operation wearing an eyeshade and a beanie with a
propeller on top.

Inevitably, prospective clients want to meet Mr. Inside to check
out the stability and reliability of the business processes.

Mr. Inside may not have a silver tongue, or the capacity to
make everyone feel special, but that's okay. His job is to
explain how his processes lower the risk for the prospect.
He doesn't need to be salesy; he only needs to be who he is:
reliable and stable.

INTRODUCE YOUR SPEAKER WITH GRACE AND SKILL

■   ■   ■

FOR CONCISE, PRECISE advice on introductions, look no further than Richard C. Borden's 1935 classic *Public Speaking as Listeners Like It*. Here, collected and condensed, are the author's inimitable insights:

1. Avoid all stale and stilted phrases such as: "It is indeed an honor . . . a man who needs no introduction."
2. Don't embarrass the speaker with extravagant promises of his oratorical brilliance.
3. Don't exaggerate your speaker's qualifications.
4. Don't give the speaker false starts like "and so I take great pleasure in introducing Ms. Paula Prolix [Ms. Prolix stands up] . . . a woman who is eminently qualified . . ." [Ms. Prolix sits back down.]
5. Don't try to steal the show by showing off your own speaking chops.

There's more to a great speech of introduction, however, than simply avoiding missteps. Answer these four simple questions briefly and skillfully, and you will create a pleasant harmony between subject, audience, occasion, and speaker:

1. Why *this subject?*
2. Why this subject *before this audience?*
3. Why this subject before this audience *at this time?*
4. Why this subject before this audience at this time *by this speaker?*

GO FOR THE GUT

■   ■   ■

ROASTING IS FRIENDLY FIRE, affectionate savagery, and public teasing. Since I grew up in a family in which teasing was practiced as fine art, let me tell you how it's done.

You find the tiniest crack in the facade of the roastee, and you drive a convoy of trucks loaded with explosives through it.

Is she self-conscious about her curly red hair? Ask her how that Brillo pad got on her head. Tell her she can do the dishes after dinner by doing a headstand in the frying pan. Tell her you'll be happy to hold her feet and *twirl*.

Is he bald and fond of his dog? Tell him he's got more dog hair on his pants than hair on his head. Ask him why he doesn't harvest the dog hair and transplant it onto his skull. Too cheap to do that? Then wear Fido as a toupee.

Get the picture? Get inside the crack and blow it open.

KEEP IT SHORT AND SWEET

■ ■ ■

THE AFTER-DINNER SPEECH should be like strawberry shortcake: short, light, and serious fun to consume.

Establish a serious theme at the outset, and then illustrate it with a whimsical story.

Remember, your audience has worked all day, talked all night, and eaten and drunk their fill. With one eye on the exit and one foot out the door, their applause will come in direct proportion to your brevity and levity.

IN SALES, SAY MORE
BY LISTENING

■　　■　　■

ONCE AGAIN, Richard C. Borden says it best in his 1935 book *Public Speaking as Listeners Like It*, "Samson slew 600 Philistines with the jawbone of an ass, and every day thousands of sales are killed with the same weapon."

In sales situations, we talk too much, don't ask enough questions, and push too hard to make the sale. We equate persuasion with talking, but what we say by listening is far more persuasive.

When we toot our own horn at the start, we consume the limited attention of the prospect. But asking questions and listening says we care, we're curious, we're willing to learn and eager to help.

And the prospect feels acknowledged, validated, understood, and happy to pay us back by listening when, at last, it's our turn to talk.

AVOID THE BEST MAN
BLUNDER

■　　■　　■

I HEARD A BEST MAN begin his toast with a story about the first time he met the groom, a tale that soon became more about the best man than his friend getting married. Within a matter of seconds, I was thinking, "All right, enough already about you. Say something nice about him."

A personal story is a good thing, but it needs to serve your purpose. If it includes details of your own colorful misadventures and derring-do traits, rewrite so it's less about you and more about the man of the hour.

You're the camera man; he's the leading man. Give *him* the close-up.

INTRODUCE YOUR*SELF*
AT A MEETING

∎ ∎ ∎

ASKED TO INTRODUCE yourself at the start of a meeting, you probably give your name and title, mention your previous jobs, and then, at the end, mention a spouse, kids, or a pet.

A string of facts has its place in the world, but when five or ten people speak their strings one after another, can you remember what anyone said? Especially if, while they were speaking, you were composing what to say when it came your turn to talk?

Once I heard a guy say, "My name is John and I am the father of twenty-six children." That got my attention, even after he explained that many of those children were foster children he had taken care of for short periods of time.

He went on to say that he'd been a CFO at four different start-ups, but that information was dwarfed by the glimpse we had of his character.

Such an approach does not conform to type, but it beats listing a string of facts about your career, and could get you heard and remembered for who you are, not what you do.

HOLD ON TO YOUR AGENDA

■   ■   ■

HENRY KISSINGER once said at a press conference,
"Does anyone have any questions for my answers?"

He meant he was going to hold on to his agenda no matter
where the press tried to take him.

Don't let the audience rewrite your talk when it's time for
Q&A. Find a way to bridge back to one of your main points no
matter where the audience wants to take you.

SPEAKING TO SENIOR DECISION MAKERS

. . .

SENIOR DECISION MAKERS are time pressed, content driven, and results oriented. They like you to be concise, fact based, and clear on the cost/benefit of your proposal.

Keep in mind that each person is trying to make a good decision based on your recommendation. While passion is an asset in many types of speaking, dispassion plays a significant role when speaking to this audience.

When one of them makes a point that could undermine your own view, it may be wise to concede the point, but then explain why it shouldn't be given too much weight in the decision-making process.

Speak with deference and link the benefits of your proposal to their strategic views.

LIGHTEN THE LOAD

■　　■　　■

HERE'S A WAY to give an upbeat talk to encourage people who face a big challenge. Start with this story: Art
Buchwald, the great humorist, once spoke to a group of lawyers, and after saying his thanks, began in this way:

> I am no stranger to the bar. I first became interested in the
> law when I was working in Paris for the *Herald Tribune*, and
> I covered a trial which had to do with a couple caught in a
> very compromising position in a Volkswagen. Now every-
> one in France was interested in the case because it had to
> do with such a small car. The judge said he didn't know if
> this was true or not so he appointed a commission to study
> it. It took them six months to render their verdict and they
> said "it was possible, but very difficult."

Then you could say, "We too are in a bit of an awkward position. And while it may be difficult for us to extricate ourselves,
it is not only possible, but certain, that we will come out of this
even stronger than we were before."

And then off you go into your plan for extrication, bringing
confidence and a light touch to what could otherwise have
been a tense situation.

USE OBSCENITIES
WITH CAUTION

■   ■   ■

RECENTLY, AT A formal event, I saw a distinguished
older man climb on a chair and use an old-fashioned four-letter
Anglo-Saxon obscenity to make a point.

I admired his daring and caught a whiff of his willfulness. He
was memorable, that's for sure, and cast himself as a guy who
would break glass to get things done.

But I'd be careful, especially during formal occasions. This guy
probably had money in the bank, was near the end of a long
career, and enjoyed playing the role of the maverick. So unless
you're like him—knee-deep in dough and roguish in character—
I suggest you dispense with foul language.

DEAL WITH DISAGREEMENT

■   ■   ■

JOHN KENNETH GALBRAITH observed, "Faced with the choice between changing one's mind and proving that there is no need to do so, almost everyone gets busy on the proof."

So, when it's decision time, and you want to change minds, listen first. Really listen. And if you're a speaker and you can't actually listen at that moment, honor the opposition by describing their point of view as they would describe it, and acknowledge what you have in common.

Then get to work on where you differ, which is most likely one, or more, of these:

> You have different positions on the issue.
> You have different ideas on how to achieve a goal.
> You have different values.

Remember, a blue speech to a red audience disappears down a black hole—unless you show that you understand before you ask to be understood.

PAINT A LASTING PICTURE

■ ■ ■

A EULOGY MUST adequately praise the virtues of the dead and give kindly exhortation to the living, urging them to emulate the finest qualities of the departed.

Name the greatest traits of the deceased. I like it when the positive traits are balanced with the shadow quality. For instance, "He was scholarly but not pedantic; funny without being silly; gentle yet highly assertive."

Tell stories that paint a picture of their virtues in action. At my mother's funeral, I told the story of how she once woke me up, in the dark of night, when I was ten, when the nearby reservoir was frozen solid. We drove to the dam, and skated for miles on black ice, with the moon shining like a brass button at the top of the sky.

It dramatized her spirit of adventure, and many people have told me they think of her often, skating in the dark, bathed in gold light.

EPILOGUE

■   ■   ■

AFTER ALL THIS TALK of dos and don'ts about framing and delivering persuasive messages, I will end with a story about Mahatma Gandhi, an Indian lawyer and political leader considered by his countrymen to be a "Great Soul" and the father of modern India.

This isn't a story I found in a book. I heard it from a man I met briefly whose earnestness made a big impression on me. He and the story have stayed with me for twenty-four years.

During the 1940s, when Gandhi sought to rid the Indian subcontinent of its British overlords and unite the various religions and castes of India, he traveled around the country by train spreading his message.

In a remote village far from the railroad, word came that Gandhi's train was coming to the district. The village elders gathered and appointed a young man of promise to make the journey of two or three days to the railhead to hear Gandhi's message and bring it back to the village.

The young man ran night and day to reach the railroad in time, only to arrive just as Gandhi's train was pulling away with the great man standing at the back of the train waving good-bye to the crowd.

Terrified that he would not live up to the expectations of his elders, that he would return to his village empty handed without a message, the young man raced after the train.

"Gandhi! Gandhi! What is your message? What is your message?" he shouted, running as the train picked up speed.

Hearing the young man's cry, and seeing the look on his face, Gandhi disappeared for an instant into the car and returned with a piece of paper, which he crumpled into a ball and threw off the back of the train.

The crumpled paper landed in the dust of the railbed where the young man found it. Kneeling down, he unfolded the paper and read:

My message is my life.

In the long run, character eats content for lunch. Who you are, who you've been, and who you are becoming send an unmistakable persuasive message—across a table, over a lectern, and even from the back of a train.

Best wishes on your journey.